AF413716

FINANCIAL LITERACY FROM A TO Z

JUSTIN BARWICK

Copyright © 2021 Justin Barwick.

ISBN: Hardcover   979-8-9853328-0-3
         Paperback   979-8-9853328-1-0
         Ebook   979-8-9853328-2-7

Contents

Message from the Author

I have been writing for as long as I can remember, dabbling in songs, poems, short stories, epic novels that were started, and many more waiting to come out. I have been wanting to write a book from start to finish for years, but I would never have thought financial literacy would be the first book I finished. But in 2020, of all years, this idea kept coming up, and a financial topic for every letter of the alphabet just kept popping up in my head. When I knew this was not going away, I started to write. While I thought this would take a while, before I knew it, half the book was written. The years in the financial industry and helping people on their financial journey really made this an easy and fun experience. Being able to educate people to help them accomplish their financial goals is a feeling that never gets old.

Of course, I also drew upon my own experiences, failures, and successes during the twenty years of my financial journey, along with fifteen years of working in the financial industry. This helped shape the direction I wanted to go and allowed me to open up more in the chapters. I believe financial literacy has become a great sound bite, but not much effort is put into it across the country. The focus in schools is not there yet, and I found many students were learning about this in college or through their own experience. Education is the most important tool we can use to help people find success in their financial journey, and I hope this book can be part of that goal.

I also want to make clear that this book is meant to provide guidance on a variety of topics, not all of which may fit with your own personal financial journey. There are numerous other subjects with which you could replace the information in the chapters, as financial literacy is more than just what's in the book. The chapters are designed to have common topics most of us can relate to along our financial journey.

There is no shame if you have ever found yourself in rough times financially. This emotion has been the most common throughout my years of working with people, but you don't have to feel that way. Any journey will have ups and downs, and how you handle these moments will determine how quickly you recover. I hope this book will help lay the foundation to get you through some of those moments with no judgment being cast. Guidance and education—not shame—is the message in the following pages.

This book has only one author, but there are many to thank for helping this become a reality. The colleagues I have worked with, especially within the college environment, who valued financial literacy as much as I have, I thank you.

My parents, who have always allowed me to dream big and encouraged me to keep writing.

Cliff, Jennifer, and Drew, who all read the first draft and responded with positive feedback while giving ideas to enhance the content.

My wife, Amanda, who has been my biggest supporter. When I came to her with this idea, she didn't hesitate to encourage me and give me the love and support to jump in. She was the rock when I doubted myself, and she believed in the book and me, even when I didn't. I will forever be grateful.

Finally, to Katie, who was the best PR professional I have ever met, and who I had the privilege to call family. She has inspired me to make the most out of each day and to live life to the fullest. I had an opportunity to make a bigger ripple in the world, and I had her behind me every day. Katie, you are missed, and I know you are proud of this book.

Attitude and Attainability

Think about a moment in your life that you were excited to start something. Maybe it was joining your first sports team or you were up for a role in a play or maybe it was your first job—anything that you were ready to start. Were you pumped up? Were you ready to dive right in and determined to be the best? The answer, hopefully, was yes, and before you even stepped foot on the field, the stage, or the office, your **attitude** was full of positivity, and you knew that you were not going to fail. I want you to hold on to that feeling because this is going to dictate how well you do with your financial plan.

When you broach the subject of financial literacy, and especially starting a budget, there's a feeling of gloom. Why is this? I think people have made it sound like it's a chore in the way they explain how to begin your financial journey. I do not think that is their intent, as most people want you to succeed because that's good for their business. The issue I come across is everything feels like an absolute, meaning, if you do not follow this plan as I have explained it, then you will not be successful. This is the blanket approach, as I like to call it, where one size fits all.

We are each our own individuals, and as such, we have different ways that we learn and approach circumstances. This is especially true when it comes to financial literacy. I know myself better than anyone because there is only one me, and with this, I know how I learn best and what works for me. When you have people telling you to do "this and that and more of this," and if you do not follow what they say, then you're doing it wrong—that's not going to work. As I stated in the beginning, the point should be: Here are ways you can get from point A to point B, and you choose which best fits your style. You can't fit a square block inside a circle, and we cannot expect each of us to learn the same way.

What I then see is people try to do everything exactly as they are taught, and if they have an *oops!* moment or it doesn't go as planned, they feel like they failed, and this resets them back to zero. I do not want to see this happen to you. My suggestion is to use the tools that you know will work for you and apply those. This will make it feel like it's been packaged specifically for you, and this will make you feel like you can do this, which you can! Know what you want on your financial journey, start with a positive attitude, and be honest with yourself. You know yourself better than anyone, and you know the best ways you can succeed.

As you continue reading, I will try my best to keep each letter of the alphabet to one word, but this next one is so important I had to speak about it.

When you make a goal for yourself, you always have an end result you are looking for, and this is where we focus our time and energy. You can see it, you can taste it, and it drives you to meet, or even exceed, your goal. Having a plan to get you to that goal is so crucial because, without one, you just have an idea with no realistic way of getting there.

Along with your plan, you must—and this is so vital—choose a goal that is **attainable**. I'm never going to play professional soccer, so it makes no sense to have this as a goal (yes, this is an extreme example, I know), but you see what I mean. If your goal is to save $5,000, and you give yourself a year to do it, and you are working ten hours a week at minimum wage, the chances of attaining the $5,000 most likely will not happen. When we make a goal, we need to make sure it's attainable and that it is written within the plan. Too many people make unrealistic financial goals, and when they do not achieve them, they feel they have failed and are less likely to try again soon. Making sure your goal is attainable will not only help you achieve success but will build confidence that you can do it. This will carry over to your next financial goal, but more importantly, will carry over to other aspects of your life. It's the psychological aspect that really makes or breaks how we do on our financial journey, and when we get a win, we feel amazing! We feel like we can do anything, and this leads to making more goals and planning for the next move. You made it happen, and no one can take that away from you.

Budget

D o I believe everyone should have a **budget**? Yes! Do I believe that the budget I use, you should use as well? I wouldn't be that bold to tell you what will work for you. You will continue to hear me say that I do not agree with the blanket approach, and my job is to go over each topic. In the end, it's your choice what you choose to use and what you do not. This is true with choosing the right budget as there are countless options, which we will go over shortly.

The main point I want to stress is you need to have some form of a budget. It makes zero sense not to know where your money is going. If your employer did not pay you the correct amount, would you say something? Of course, you would; it's your money! Would you pay the wrong price at the store if the sign says something different? No, of course, you wouldn't; it's your money! Why do we not take this same approach each month when our money is going out as fast as it is deposited? You should want to know where every dollar goes so you can see if your choices are benefiting your financial plan or stalling them. It's your money!

Why have a budget? Like I stated previously, you should want to know where your money is going. No matter the overall reason for your budget, whether it's to lower debt, find out if you're paying too much on certain bills like cable (if this is still as relevant), a cell phone plan, or putting money aside for future endeavors, you need to see where your money is going. When I have met with people and reviewed where their money was going, they always been shocked to learn how much they overspend, especially on eating out.

I reviewed a budget for a couple I have known for a long time. As we looked at money to be used to eat out, I noticed that over $600 was spent at a restaurant that is known for having very good deals on food and happy hour all day. The point is you really have to try to spend a lot of money at this establishment. When I pointed this out, it was a look of shock because money was tight with them, and just cutting this in half would help immensely. Now, the budget will show you where your money is going, but you have to be the one to make the change. This is the number one reason to have a budget: to know where your money is going. Remember, it's your money!

You're ready to start your budget, but which one should you choose? Well, that's going to be up to you. What budget works best with your learning style? You can find budgets in Excel, Google to find various options, check with your financial institution (as most have online budgets to use). There are options on your phone with many companies coming up with apps, so finding the best option will not be too difficult. There are a few things to remember: 1) make sure the first budget accounts for your current financial needs; 2) your budget will change based on your financial journey, so be ready to make changes where needed; 3) account for all money coming in and going out each month; 4) and last but not least, have a section for your savings. We will talk more about this in a later chapter.

The next question I get is what should my budget look like at month's end? Again, there are different thoughts to this, and I will share a few I have come across that have been successful. The first is to have all money accounted for, and you are left with zero dollars at the end of the month. You have allocated all of your funds into each category, so not even one cent is unaccounted for.

Another option is to have money left over after allocating your funds for the month, always leaving a surplus. I like this technique because I see it as a game, and the goal is to have more funds left than what I spent (savings is included). This allows you to challenge yourself to really try to not overspend, which, if you are new to budgeting, may not be the best option to start until you become more consistent.

The next two really focus on either lowering debt or saving. You can direct your budget to focus heavily on your debt where you pay the necessities first (home, utilities, etc.), the items you need to survive on. Whatever is left over (after allocating into savings), you can throw onto that debt. The reverse I have seen is at the start of your budget, you put a percentage, or dollar amount, into savings to start. From there, the remainder of the funds you can use as you see fit. This ensures savings is the number one priority. Both of these are good options if you're up for the challenge.

In the end, the best budgeting option is what works best for your current financial situation. You decide where you need to focus on and choose the budget that parallels this. I am sure there are other ways to look at your budget than those I have shared, but my job is to give you ideas that I have seen work. But like I said previously, the blanket effect does not apply here, so choose what works best for you. Remember, this could change in the future, so it's good to know what options make sense for you. The end result is you have started budgeting your money and know where it's going (and where you need it to go), and this is a big step to you succeeding in your financial journey.

It's your money!

Credit

This word elicits so many different emotions based on how this has affected you. So what does your **credit** really mean? Your credit shows how risky financial institutions see you in regard to lending you money. The higher your score, the better chance you have of securing a loan at a low-interest rate. If you have a lower score, you may have an uphill battle to be approved, and if you are approved, you could be looking at a higher interest rate.

If you let someone borrow money with the expectation they will pay you back, you would be cautious who you lent to, correct? The same holds true for a financial institution, except there are numbers they use to help determine the amount of risk. The credit bureaus that help determine your credit score are Equifax, Experian, and Transunion. You should have heard of at least one of these. I was always taught that Equifax is used for the eastern part of the United States, Experian for the Midwest, and Transunion for the western part. Mortgage loans will take all of these into account, which we will discuss later.

What do you need to do to raise your credit and ensure you are a low risk? Education, education, education (which happens to be a chapter) is critical to your success. Understanding where the pitfalls are would have helped many people from failing when they started their credit. Here are some quick tidbits of advice:

Pay your bills on time! This is so simple and yet is still a major issue. Always pay at least your minimum monthly payments. If you are more than thirty days late, this could impact your score by as many as 70 points.

That's a huge blow, especially if you have been working on your credit. If it's still on the low side, it won't hurt as much, but the lender will want to know why you were unable to make your payment. This also includes your bills such as utilities, cell phone, cable, etc. These do not help your credit, although there's been conversation to include these, especially with students. Some lenders do take into consideration that if you are more than thirty days late, it will show up negatively on your credit. And this will again hurt your score. The first thing you do after educating yourself is *do not be late!*

Credit Card Utilization. For many of us, our first time dipping our toes in the credit pool is with a credit card (although student loans are also on this list). Let's say you receive a card with a credit limit of $1,000, and you follow the rule of paying your bills on time each month. You're off to a great start. You also want to ensure you're not carrying a balance of more than 30 percent of your utilization, meaning any balance over $300 you carry over month to month will negatively impact your score. This is almost like a siren is going off to warn you if you continue to pile on debt, then your score will take a hit, and we want to avoid this.

Each of the credit bureaus will have educational links to explain these and more about what makes up your credit score. There's lots of very good information, and I encourage you to look further at each site as the information is invaluable and comes from direct sources.

I did want to bring up one more topic about credit that I get asked, which is: Should I even have credit? There are people who firmly believe that you do not need credit because that leads to debt, which leads to financial hardships—which can be difficult to get out of. You should use cash, and you do not need credit. They're not wrong. You can do these things and not build credit while using cash on your financial journey. But as I have said a few times already, this does not mean this is the best advice for you and your situation.

I happen to believe in building my credit and using it when I need to. When I plan a trip, I put it on my credit card, which gets me points, and I pay it off immediately. I've already saved the cash and have allocated it to my trip. Why not get some points off for my next trip, whether it be flights, hotels, or other perks? We just purchased all new kitchen appliances, and I used my card that has 0.00% interest. I will have it paid off and will not need cash to pay for it right now. This works for me. Building your credit will allow you to take advantage of special rates if you choose to do so. But maybe this is not for you, and that's okay. What works for my financial journey does not have to be what works for you, but the more you put into your financial literacy, the better chance you have to make your credit work for you.

Debt

We can all agree, no matter how you approach financial literacy, that having too much **debt** is not a good thing. In fact, debt leads down many negative roads if not handled the right way. If you are just starting your financial journey, and have no debt, then it's critical you learn as much as possible about what affects your credit and the areas that people get in trouble. If you have some debt but have handled it well, then this will serve as a reminder and offer tips to continue on your solid path. If you have made some *oops!* moments with your credit, this will serve to help you back to the road of financial redemption. Here are a few things to consider:

Understand the product. Know what you are getting into. If you are getting a credit card, you should know the interest rate, annual fees, due date, and any bonuses for using the card. Are you getting a 0% introductory rate, and if you miss a payment (which you shouldn't), will this end the 0% rate? Store credit cards have been the ones I hear the most about because they get you right when you are purchasing and tell you that you can save 10% or 20% now with a store card. Sounds like a deal, right? The person in front of you is trying to hit a sales goal and may not be able to answer the questions above, leaving you with debt that you originally were not prepared to take on. When you take on a loan, you need to be able to ask all the questions you can and have them answered, not handed some booklet and wait for your card to come in the mail. There are great sites online that will help compare cards and most loans so you can have a better understanding before you jump in.

Know your budget. As we discussed, your budget will tell you what you can and cannot afford. Use it! Even if you are approved for more than you budgeted, it doesn't mean you have to take it. The goal for most financial institutions is to get as high a dollar amount as they can approve to meet their numbers. As long as the number fits into their procedure, they're good to go. If you have purchased a car, you most likely have been asked, "What monthly payment are you looking for?" This is so they can work with their partners to find that monthly payment no matter what the length of the loan may be. Unfortunately, most people are not looking out for your benefit, so it's up to you to use your budget and know what you want; this takes away their power and increases yours. At the end of the day, you're responsible for the debt, so make sure you can handle it.

Take what you need. This can apply to almost every loan, and we just spoke about this briefly. Just because you were approved for a higher amount does not mean you need it. The two types of loans about which I hear this the most are credit cards and student loans. The credit card is different because you only pay for what you spend, plus interest, meaning you can control this to an extent. However, if you do not have a budget and instead of the $500 limit, you get $2,500, you could get yourself into a hole quickly. Revolving debt—meaning you pay what you borrow and what you pay toward principal goes back for you to use again—can get you into trouble if you use it and do not have a plan to pay it.

Student loans are different because they are a term loan. This means that what you borrow, you cannot borrow any longer from that loan, and you pay it over a specific period. There are benefits with student loans, such as deferment of payment until six months after you graduate to lower interest rates, but you must only take what you need. Even with a deferred payment, interest could still be accumulating dependent on the type of student loan, and this is still debt you owe. By owing a lot of debt with no plan to pay it off, you could end your college career, and this may not include a graduate program. Once you agree to take a loan, you are responsible for repaying the loan as you are the only one looking out for yourself.

Education, Education, Education

This may be the most important chapter as I firmly believe the more we educate ourselves in financial literacy, the better chance we have to make the right decisions for ourselves—not let someone else tell us what to do based on their own needs. Too many times, I have heard people tell me they did not fully understand what they were getting into. "The car was beautiful, and I really couldn't afford it, but they gave me a longer-term loan, possibly up to seven years!" or "The credit card limit was more than I asked, but they told me not to worry about it and just use what you need to"—not realizing it's hard to control your spending when it's so easy to use.

There are those who will put the blame on you for not realizing what you're signing up for, and to an extent, that may be true. But looking at my own experiences and what many have told me throughout the year, education was the disconnect between starting your credit on a positive note and starting it already in the hole. We tend to start paying more attention once we have that *oops!* moment and are now climbing out of that hole. And, of course, we are made to feel guilty that we caused this on our own. But why is this the case? I think there are a number of contributing factors, but the main one is lack of financial **education** in schools.

You may get an economics class in high school, and this may be an elective but not a requirement. So you could literally go through twelve grades of school without financial literacy even being brought up. That is unbelievable! Many times, financial literacy is first introduced in college. Everyone is not in the same situation, and this is not always the case, it's just what I have experienced and heard through my years working with people.

How do we change this trend? Introducing financial literacy at an earlier age would be a great start. There are solid organizations that teach about money as early as elementary school, so there's a foundation. Financial literacy should be a requirement at high school at the very least. Financial literacy shouldn't be looked at as an elective because it affects everyone. We all have our own financial journeys, and money, credit, savings, and debt are all part of this, so why is this pushed in the background? Until we put financial literacy right next to the core subjects students are consistently tested on, we will continue to have financial issues.

Now that I have gotten down from my soapbox, how can you learn more about your credit? I have a few options where you can start, so go with what you feel comfortable with. Remember, this is about *your* financial journey.

School Partnerships. If your school happens to partner with a student banking provider, this is a great place to start, and hopefully, your school chose the partner because they were there to provide financial literacy first and foremost. When I worked with the student partnerships, our mission was to spread financial literacy on campus, no matter if you were a client or not. I knew for many students this would be their first experience with this topic, and I wanted to ensure it started off positively (attitude played a big part). We partnered with departments on campus to work towards creating an environment that paralleled the mission of student success. There were live workshops, online tutorials—anything we felt would better the students' financial journey, we wanted to be there. I'm not saying every banking partner has this mission, but they should. The more we educate people on the importance of their finances, the better prepared they will be, and because your organization was there for them, they will be loyal to you because you cared about their financial journey when many did not.

Financial Institutions. This should be obvious, but it's not always so. Yes, financial institutions are there to make money, and that's fine. They are a business. However, as I stated above, if you do the right thing by educating your clients instead of just trying to get them approved no matter what, you will have loyal clients for life, and you will reap the benefits in the long run. All financial institutions offer pretty much the same products, and there's not too much variance from place to place, so what sets them apart? It's their service and how they can help you with your financial journey, not their bottom line. If you walk into your financial institution and they don't seem willing to take the time to educate you, then it's time to look elsewhere. There's too much to lose by making the wrong financial decisions.

University Resources. I failed miserably on this as I did not seek, understand, or know about financial resources when I was in school. Of course, I do not think they were promoted as much as they are now, but I didn't even take the time to try, so that's on me. Ask what your university offers for financial literacy and see what classes, online courses, or speakers provide the information you want. If your university is light on these offerings, then get involved and push to make this a focus. Student success isn't just about graduating, it's about preparing you for all aspects of life after graduation, and your financial journey is just as important.

Family/Friends. If your family has been successful with their financial journey and can provide the education you need, then that's great news and allows you to be ahead of the curve. Unfortunately, many do not have this and instead learn what not to do (hopefully) or fall into the same trap. Anytime family or friends give advice, ask yourself: *Would I trust this person to pay me back if I lent them money?* It doesn't make them bad people if you say no; it just means they were never educated on the importance of financial literacy. You would be amazed at how much you can help others once you have your financial journey on the right path. It is impossible to reach every single person, but if you take something out of this book, then you could pass on the knowledge to someone else, and this is what really gets the message moving.

Financial Institutions

T his will be a brief chapter since we touched on this in the previous one. For most of us, we will use a **financial institution** at some time in our life, whether it be opening a checking or savings account, for lending needs, or investments. Our 401ks are with a financial firm, and almost all things we pay for have some attachment to a financial institution. So what do we need to know?

We already learned the financial products offered are very similar, so not too much of a difference. Interest rates usually are not too far apart, so that may not be a good separation tactic. Service, now that is one that separates the good from the bad. Are your needs their priority, or are you seen as a number that occasionally provides them with ways to meet their goals? The job of the banker is to find what your financial needs/goals are and offer financial solutions that meet these needs. The key is YOUR financial needs. When you find that this is their mission, then you have the right place. Of course, just because the mission states this does not mean the individual you are speaking to believes this. This is why it's so important to begin your financial literacy earlier rather than later. You want to prevent being placed into a financial solution that is not the best fit or is not the best fit right now but could be in the future. Know the mission of your financial institution and be the one to interview them. After all, they are there to serve your financial needs, not the other way around. They should be earning your business every day.

Financial institutions are great in the beginning, and they really try to offer as many financial solutions as they can. You walk away thinking, *Yeah, they really are looking out for me.* This is great, and I know there are many people who can relate. It's an amazing experience. I want this for everyone; however, there are just as many people who feel they are shown the world when they first open their accounts, and then there is no more contact. No more offering of services, no more feeling like they are the only customer. They almost feel like they are a burden to the employees. All those amazing financial solutions were offered, most likely a sales quota, and now that they feel you don't qualify for anything more, it's time to move on. This is why it's important to do your homework before choosing a financial institution and understand how they operate. You need a financial partner that will help you prepare for your first home and what you need to have ready, not one that wants you to figure it out on your own and then come to them when you are ready, just so they can add to their quota. You are more than an account number, and you need to be somewhere that believes the same.

I plan to write a book on financial institutions and knowing when it's time to find a new one. I believe this will help you understand the signs when it's time to move on. Like everything we speak about in this book, education will be the key to a successful financial journey.

Groceries/Going Out

This is one of the budget topics that gets a lot of conversations—food! I need a G, and so **groceries** and **going out** seemed to work very well!

The amount of money we spend on food is a lot, and it's an area where I see the most waste. How often do you go to the grocery store, buy food, and then throw out expired items? I would guess quite a bit, and I, unfortunately, have done this many times as well. I am much better, but there are times it still happens. Does that make you a bad person? No. Does it mean you just throw your money away? No. It just means you need a better plan, and a budget would help you plan your money better.

If you are going to the store with no real plan in mind, you might buy what you do not need. Stores are designed to maximize your spending and hope you want to go up each aisle and shop with your eyes (or stomach if you have not eaten yet). To counter this, start with your budget and find out the amount you can spend on groceries each month. Once you have a dollar amount, what food do you need? Set a schedule of meals for the week and buy only what you need. Now, if you don't have the budget to buy steaks, sea bass, and champagne, don't do it! Most of us do not have the ability to do this each week, and that's okay. Look at the weekly specials, come up with a plan of attack, and then shop. Your wallet will thank you, and you'll have a whole week of food. Every once in a while, you should treat yourself. Just make sure you follow your budget.

Once you have your grocery plan in place, you are good to go, correct? Well, if you only stay in to eat, then you probably will be fine; however, many of us like to go out to eat. We feel we should be able to treat ourselves and let someone else do the cooking. We've worked hard all week, right? There is absolutely nothing wrong with wanting to go out to eat. You just have to make it part of your budget. Groceries and going out should be two separate line items on your budget. I have seen people put it under one, and it becomes a mess. Not to say you couldn't do this; just remember you know what works best for you.

How often do you go out? Once a month? Once a week? Every day? And where do you go? Fancy places or quick takeout? Do you order drinks as well? These are all questions to know when you are calculating your budget, and based on how you work, your budget will determine the amount. Since going out is a want and not a necessity, make sure your budget needs are met before even entering a dollar amount.

Plus, if you just spent money on groceries, do you need to go out? You don't want to spend money on groceries just to go out and eat and spend roughly the same amount. I have read that food should be around 10% of your budget (groceries and going out), and some have dollar amounts of around $250 per adult, and these are good measures. But you are your own person, and you need to decide what works for your budget. The best I can suggest is to buy what you know you will eat and treat yourself when you can. Just make sure you have it within your budget to do so.

Here's an example where you can make your groceries work for you. If you go out to eat and order steak, you can expect to be charged between $25 and $50 (yes, I know, depending on where you go, these prices can vary). For this exercise, let's say it's $32 for a steak, and we will include two sides. You have someone with you who orders the same as you. Now you're at $64 just for the food. And from my experience, the steaks may not seem as big as you would like. Now, after tax and tip, and let's say you only ordered water, you're looking at around $82 total.

You can purchase a whole beef tenderloin when it's on sale. I usually look for it when it's $9.99 a pound. I did it for the first time recently, got it just above six pounds, and after cutting it up, I had seven filets, and the rest was ground up to use later. Now, this isn't for everyone, but for less than the price of the meal above, you would have three of these plus additional meat for another meal or two. This is another example of how eating at home will almost always be cheaper than going out. This is not to say you shouldn't. My wife and I enjoy going out and trying new places, but this is the exception, not the rule. We eat at home more often as we have adhered to our budget and going out is planned so we know what the cost will be. Your budget should allow you to enjoy life; just make sure you plan so you're not regretting that costly night out.

Let's take a cheaper option than steak that we can use. You're craving pasta and your energy level is at zero so going out is the only solution. That's fine you have the funds budgeted to do so. You order pasta bolognese which is just sauce with meat in it. Simple dish and can run between $12-$20 depending on where you go. Not a high priced meal and a go to for me if I am craving pasta. But, if you bought the ingredients and made it at home you would be saving money and have leftovers if you used everything. Pasta costs around $2.50 and many times it's a BOGO (buy one get one) and a jar of sauce runs around $3 with ground beef around $3-$4. Let's keep this generic and you're buying the supermarket brand which tends to be cheaper and usually tastes just as good, you're looking at around $8.50. Might not seem like a huge difference but if you got a deal where it's BOGO then this has already made it a bargain and you'll most likely have leftovers that can be another meal or two. And it's pretty quick to prepare too!

These are just a couple of examples of food that are popular in restaurants. You can enjoy many foods from the comfort of your home for far less money. By looking for deals, using coupons, and not shopping at only one supermarket, you can buy affordable groceries. With all the sites out there to help you, I believe almost anyone can make a good meal for far less than what they spend going out to eat.

Habit

Why am I writing this book? My main objective is to help you conquer your financial journey, especially in the areas you feel you need help with. It's also to help you form better habits with your money so it becomes second nature. Have you heard of the 21/90 rule? It states it takes 21 days to make a **habit** and 90 days to make it part of your life. Now I can assure you people could argue with this, and in certain examples, I may do so as well. The point is not always the numbers but being consistent in what you are trying to accomplish. Take a budget, for example. If you adhere to it each day, week, and month, the likelihood of this becoming part of your financial journey becomes greater. You can see the results, and this, in turn, provides confidence. Many of these chapters deal with our confidence in seeing positive results, and when we understand the pitfalls and how this can really impact us financially, we tend to continue the habit.

I think of instances where I needed to form habits and took the time to be consistent. When I got to college, I had to relearn how to study because, up to then, I didn't have to put in as much effort. As I progressed with more difficult classes and not having the structure I did at home, I realized if I did not make a change, my grades would suffer. So I had to carve out time each week to study and maintain those times on a consistent basis. If I did not form this new habit, I risked failing my classes and the potential to not remain at my university. The consequences were severe, and I had to make a decision. Thankfully, I realized the habit would make a positive change compared to the other option. Your financial journey is similar; the habits you form will shape how your journey goes and how quickly you will reap the benefits. It won't be easy, but it will be worth it.

I used to hear it takes 10,000 hours of practice to become an expert (from Malcolm Gladwell's book *Outliers*), and this seems to hold true for athletes, musicians, actors—anything where we are performing a skill. Now, I have never tested this theory in terms of the total number of hours, but when I played hockey, the more time I spent working on my skating, shooting, and puck handling, the better I became until I reached the point to where it became second nature.

Now, I won't say you need this many hours to be an expert with your finances, as we are all different and have different goals. But our financial journey never goes away, and we live and breathe it every day, so in reality, many of us will spend more than 10,000 hours learning this skill. We will spend every day looking at our finances because we are using them every day. It's an ever-flowing concept and can change based on many factors that could include a job change, starting a relationship, being part of a retirement program, even going out to eat. Our financial journey will always be there, even if we try to ignore it. The goal of this book is to get you better prepared so the journey becomes enjoyable instead of something you dread. The more you know, the better off you will be.

Identity Theft/Fraud

"It's not if it will happen, it's when." This was said in a workshop I attended that was led by an FBI agent, and it really hit home. We hear about so many breaches with major retailers, city governments, even one of the credit bureaus, so it makes sense that at some point in time, we will be affected by some form of **identity theft** or **fraud**.

We live in a world that has become more digital, and we do so many things online like shopping, banking, investing, meeting people—you name it, it's probably online. And this is a great thing because the convenience allows us to be able to do these things when we may not have the time to be physically present. On the other hand, it does expose us more to potential traps that could steal information that could impact our finances. Even before we moved to a more digital lifestyle, we were taught to be cautious of our surroundings, and the same holds true in the digital landscape. Are these foolproof ideas that will stop every potential breach? No, because sometimes it's beyond our control, but there are precautions we can take to hopefully keep our information safe and limit the impact when a situation occurs. I am not going to wander into the conversation of how much of our information is already out there, such as our social security numbers. I believe that is an area that I do not have the knowledge or understanding of what this actually looks like. I am more concerned about the everyday things we can do.

Credit Reports. If you are not reviewing your credit reports once a year, then you need to start right now. You are entitled to review your credit reports from each of the credit bureaus—Equifax, Experian, and TransUnion—once a year for free, and one great site is freecreditreport.com. This does not mean you will see your score; it just means you can see if there are any tradelines (any debt you have is called a tradeline) that isn't yours. If you see something that does not look right, you can dispute with that credit bureau to protect your credit and your information. You have been vigilant with your money, and you need to be just as vigilant with your credit. This also allows you to see what might be affecting your credit, such as high revolving credit utilization (credit cards), length of credit, and what debt you can start to pay off to improve your credit. Everybody is always concerned about the credit score, but you can pretty much have a good idea where you are based on your credit report.

What if you see something that's on there that shouldn't be, and you successfully get this taken off, but you want to do more to protect yourself? You can always have that credit bureau put a freeze on your credit, meaning anytime you go to have your credit pulled for a loan, you have to contact the credit bureau to unfreeze your credit so the financial system can run your report. I've seen many people do this to allow them the peace of mind that if someone does try to use their information, they have put a barrier to those criminals. There are also credit protection agencies that monitor your credit for a monthly fee. They alert you if someone tries to run your credit and usually have monetary compensation if your identity is hacked. I have had this service for a while because it gives me peace of mind, and my family has used this as well. I am not here to tell you the service I use as I believe you should not be influenced by me. I will say there are a few large companies that would be your best bet, as they have a history to review, and people will let you know their experiences. This is not for everyone, but again, it's important you know what is out there.

Credit Cards and Debit Cards. We tend to purchase more online than at any other time, and we need to be sure we protect our information regarding our money. When making a purchase, please make sure you are familiar with this company and not clicking on a random site that says they have great deals on sunglasses that you have never heard of. There's a good chance this could compromise your card information. Your credit card provider should have protection should a purchase be made that was not authorized by you. Since the credit card is not attached to your personal banking account, you can put the card aside and wait until this matter has been settled, the funds are back on the card, and you have your new credit card in the mail. But what if your debit card is compromised and the amount has really affected you paying your bills, groceries, or other needed expenses? There are a couple of ways to help minimize the damage as your finances could take up to ten business days to resolve (it's usually much quicker, but each case is different).

Don't Put Your Eggs in One Basket. Allocate your funds so if a debit card is compromised, it only affects the checking account attached to the card. If you shop online often, then have an account strictly for online usage. This way, if you are compromised, you have your other accounts to continue purchasing the every-day things you need. You don't need ten accounts but keeping one account for possible riskier transitions could be a smart move. Now, there are plenty of cases where someone's credit card was compromised at a retail store they walked into. This is where a savings account comes in handy, and you should have a good amount kept separate from your checking account so you do not spend all of your money. (Remember that budget chapter?) Immediately shut down your card (your financial institution may have already done this) and get a new one ordered right away. Don't think about the worst-case scenario, but be prepared so that if it happens, the damage is minimized.

Do Not Give Away Your Information. There is no prince that is willing to give you millions of dollars. There is no foreign lottery you won in a country you have never set foot in. No one would send you a check to deposit and ask that you send them back part of it, letting you can keep the rest. These are scams and will do nothing but allow you the privilege to owe your financial institution money when your account goes negative. If it sounds too good to be true, it probably is, especially when it comes to money. At one point, there might have been something you read that sounded enticing but some force in your gut held you back. That was probably a very good thing because the consequence would have been damaging and could have set your budget back quite a bit. You work hard for your money and wouldn't just give it away; the same is true for these scams.

Bank Information. Your financial institution will never email or call you for your private information. We do not have any system updates that require you to log in from an email. Their job is to protect your information and your passwords are for your use; they do not want to know what those are. This has hit many good people who thought they were doing the right thing and allowed access to their online banking. If this happens, the first thing you want to do is change your online ID and password. If you feel there may be an issue with your computer, then you need to get it cleaned to look for any malignant programs that could be stealing your information. I would advise not saving your passwords and possibly use a VPN service but look for ways you are comfortable with to protect your information. The more we use our devices, the more important protecting our information will be.

Joint Borrowers

This is an extremely important chapter, and if you do not understand what this means, then this chapter is for you. This chapter could be your saving grace to maintain your credit.

When you apply for a loan—let's say it's an auto loan—you sometimes cannot get approved on your own. Maybe it's your credit, or your debt to income (more than 45% of your income is going towards outstanding debt), or the vehicle is more than you probably can afford. In such cases, you may be asked to add a **joint borrower** (also known as a co-borrower or cosigner). Now, if you have someone that can mitigate any of the risks mentioned through their credit, income, and low debt, then you'd be pretty happy. Your interest rate will probably be much lower based on the joint borrower's credit score. You both sign the paperwork, you have the new vehicle, and life could not be any better. Of course, you will make the payments and reassure the joint borrower that this will be the case. And I hope this is what happens and everyone lives happily ever after.

But what if it doesn't, and let's say *you* are the joint borrower? Are you aware that you are equally responsible for the debt? That even though the other borrower is actually driving the car, if they stop paying, it also affects *your* credit? Too many times, people have told me their credit was messed up by being a joint borrower on a loan. The other person was not paying, and they had no idea until the notices came in. Or they went to apply for a loan and were denied because there was a tradeline that showed delinquency. You can explain to the loan officer the whole situation, and we will empathize with you; however, once your credit was pulled to be a joint borrower, the debt was now yours as well.

Now, we may think that the joint borrower was a good friend, or maybe they had been dating for a while and should have known better since they were not married or were family. I'm here to tell you from my own experience that family members and spouses tend to get into the most trouble. We want to trust people closest to us and believe that they would never do anything that could hurt us financially. Unfortunately, this isn't always the case. I have heard of people having family members sign as joint borrowers on student loans only to never pay them again. Or car loans where payments just stopped coming in, and there was no response from the person driving the car. Or people who spend recklessly and figure they will make it up next month.

The issue comes in that after thirty days, your credit will be hit, and it will be a large number, possibly up to 70 points. There are some people who will say anything to get what they want, and they may not be responsible with their money, yet we potentially sign a document that could cost us our credit that we have worked so hard on. Plus, it can hit your accounts as you will end up paying more on interest when your score goes down, and this is not on your report.

How do you know if the person you trust is really responsible? I am sure there have been signs in the past with their money habits, and we usually just let it slide. Plus, they would never put a family member in that position. I am fortunate enough to have a wife who I trust to make her payments on a loan we are on because we share the same goal of wanting to make the best life we can for both of us—and we budget. For me, the best advice I can give is this: Would you lend the person in front of you a large sum of money and expect to be paid back as agreed upon? This is a hard question and one I have used because this is what I asked myself when I have fought to get a loan approved. If I say yes, which does not happen often, then I have said the risk posed by this person is small, and I feel confident of being paid back. Now, this is with strangers, but I ask the same with people I know very well, and there is only a handful I would say yes to. We will speak about this more in the marriage chapter. At the end of the day, you must feel comfortable in the decision you make with your money, and this is just to allow you to see what could happen. It doesn't mean it will, but as I have said many times, the more educated you are, the better decisions you make for your financial journey and no one else.

Kids

This chapter is not going to be about preparing yourself for **kids** or having the right plan so you know you can afford the expenses that come along with this. One, I am not a parent as of right now and would never be so bold as to tell you what you should do as I have said previously. Two, life happens, and many times, we may not be ready at that exact moment, and that's okay. This is what makes life exciting—the unknown. Life-changing events can feel less frightening when you have consistent habits with your money and you are focused on your financial journey, so no matter what happens, you can adapt. This is such a huge ability in so many facets of our lives.

When we spoke about budgets, we said they are ever-changing, almost like a life form in how they can evolve. Moments can shift which direction you need to go or where you need to focus more on. Not just in your day-to-day life but also in your budget. By paying yourself first, educating yourself on credit, and making sure you are making financial decisions based on your needs, you will be able to financially tackle having a child. I speak from conversations I have had with family members and the realization and happiness once they find out are now how we are going to support the child. The hospital is just the first step in the financial planning of having a child.

Does one parent take more time from work to be there? (This discussion tends to lead to which countries have more time for the parents, and that is another subject we will not be getting involved in.) How much does a nanny or daycare cost? When should we start a college fund? What will our grocery bill look like? You now have someone who depends on you for everything, and you want to make sure you can provide financially. By taking your financial journey seriously, you will be able to handle this and adjust your budget. That trip overseas will need to wait or going out will not be a priority for a long time. You will be able to allocate funds to the areas you feel are necessary to what you will need to provide to your child. This could even mean looking at a larger place to live as your family grows.

The important thing to realize is you are having a baby, and that's exciting! You have been diligent with your finances that after reviewing your budget and researching costs for planning to bring your child home, you are able to allocate funds from different buckets to the areas you know will be vital when you are ready to bring your child home. Money can make even the happiest moments fill you with stress, and I want to help you avoid this at all costs. If this is the one lesson you get, then I have done my job. Work on your budget, allow it to evolve, make sure you are putting money away, and the happy moments will continue to be what they should be: happy moments.

Leasing

This chapter will focus on **leasing** a car and not an apartment or any other type of lease.

The debate between buying and leasing a car continues to go on with many very opposed to the other side. Many people feel leasing a vehicle is a waste of money and that you are dumb if you do so. We will break it down a bit more, but I need to clarify my position as I have done throughout the book. The decision is up to you and what's best for you. No one should be telling you what you should do and making you feel that you're somehow a fool for leasing. If you have budgeted correctly and leasing is the option you prefer, then that's the right option for you. Too many times, people are shamed for leasing, and as you know, we are all different. Our financial decisions need to be what works best for ourselves and no one else. Now that we continue to be in a no-judgment zone, let's talk a bit more about leasing versus buying.

When you lease a vehicle, you are essentially renting the car for a set amount of time, usually between two to three years. You will have a monthly car payment, and money is usually asked for up front. You can negotiate to have these tied into your monthly payments. Once the term is up to return the car, you can either purchase it (lease buyout), look for another lease, or choose to purchase another vehicle. For those who consistently lease, the first question asked is, "Why do you lease knowing you're always going to have a car payment?" If you tend to be the type to purchase a vehicle, this question will baffle you, and some financial experts have just told you that's the dumbest thing to do. So why do people lease? From people I have spoken to, it comes down to three things:

1. *"I like having a new car every few years."* Many people get bored with their vehicles and like having a new one as often as possible.

2. *"Payments are lower with a lease."* In today's market, car loans can have pretty high monthly payments, and people feel that leasing provides them with a better alternative for a more cost-efficient monthly payment. Many people cannot afford a 36-month loan. However, a 36-month lease is far more affordable.

3. *"I don't have to deal with any out-of-pocket expenses."* If something does go wrong with the vehicle, the dealership most likely will be able to repair it without you having to pay out of pocket. Now, if it's your error that causes damage, that could be another story, but because

you actually do not own the vehicle, the maintenance costs are much lower.

So why do people feel so strongly against leasing? They see it as a never-ending car payment, you never own the asset, you can only drive a certain amount of miles during the lease period, and you are putting money down for the pleasure of driving a car that will never be yours (unless you purchase at the end). These are all valid points, and they do make sense. In the end, it's about what you want and if you budget a certain amount for your vehicle, then decide what is best for you. I can tell you that I like to own my vehicle and have driven the same one for over ten years and have owned it for about five years now (if you are reading this in the distant future, I may have broken down and purchased another one). I like having the asset and look to pay off the loan as soon as possible (I really like the biweekly payment options to cut the loan down quicker and get an extra payment each year). This is what works best for me.

My wife, on the other hand, leases her vehicle for the reason described above. She bought a car when we first started dating, and it just wasn't for her. She likes having a new vehicle every few years, and her car payment has stayed around the same even though we budget higher to make sure it fits into our budget. She feels that if she were to buy again, then leasing lets her really be able to commit to a vehicle. We are completely on the other side of this issue, and we have learned why the other does what they do. In the end, I would never demean my wife in her decision to lease because it's her vehicle, and she needs to do what she is comfortable with. We make sure the budget reflects this and that we look for the best deals on the vehicle she is looking to lease. You can still negotiate a lease even if people feel you cannot. My sister-in-law was a professional with negotiating her leases and always walked away with a much lower car payment, with extra services added on while driving vehicles that are considered more expensive. So I could do what many people would on my side of the argument and tell her every reason why this is dumb and how this makes no sense and end up having an argument over a vehicle she will be driving. Or we work together to budget for the vehicle, understand why she prefers leasing, and let her make the decision since it's what's best for her. She has never once made me feel dumb for buying a vehicle, and I would never do that to her.

Like many of the topics we are discussing, when it comes to your financial journey, you have to choose what works best for you. If you budget correctly, put money aside for your savings, and work towards your retirement, then you can decide whether you are going to be a buyer of cars or a leaser. There isn't a right or wrong way, only the one you decide is best for you. Too many times, we are belittled for our financial decisions, and what financial institutions should be looking at is what was just stated. If you plan properly, educate yourself on the options, then the decision you make will be the correct one. The person telling you that you made the wrong decision does not live your life and is not you—no one knows you better than you!

Marriage

There is a good chance that most of you will enter into some form of a commitment with someone, whether it be through **marriage**, partnership, or anything where you are sharing your life with another person. In a perfect world, the love you have for each other would be able to solve any problem that revolves around finances. However, that is not the case. When you commit yourself to someone, especially in the legal sense, you are not just sharing your lives together but the financial aspect as well. Does your partner have a good credit score? Are they a saver or a spender? Do they budget, or even know what a budget looks like? Do they come into the relationship with financial baggage, meaning a load of debt? Unfortunately, these are questions to know the answers to because you could be sharing your financial journey with someone with the complete opposite thinking of you. And unless you can work together to ensure either you both are on the same journey or make a plan to work through this issue, there will be future arguments that may never be resolved.

Finances can destroy a marriage if not discussed early, so both of you should know what each brings to the table and agree on the direction you want your lives to go. It may not be an easy conversation, and people tend to be defensive when they have made financial mistakes, and the people who are financially sound tend to be accusatory. Here is the number one rule to follow when you have the conversation: understand the why and work from there. If you do the exact opposite of what I have been trying to say in regards to understanding how someone got to where they are in their finances, then they will just see you as another person putting them down for mistakes made. Instead, find out why. I can bet that financial education is the culprit, whether it be with companies not explaining what they were getting into or they were a product of their environment where finances were never discussed. You chose to be with this person for a reason, so take the time to better understand how you can work together to build the life you want and both be successful on your financial journey.

My wife is more of the spender, and I am more of the saver, planning for the future. We definitely had discussions early on about our finances when there was more debt than we should have had and we were not making a conscious effort to save. We were living our lives just fine, but we knew we were spending too much on debt, more on going out, and hardly any on savings. Except for her pension and my 401k, we were not prepared if an emergency arose. Just because one person tends to be the spender does not mean it all falls on them. I was not properly following my own advice and knew something had to be done.

The first thing I did was look over our debt, mainly credit cards, and figure out a plan to pay these off. Once I had my personal debt together, I made a plan to consolidate and pay it off. I did let my wife know what I was doing because that's the right thing, and it let her see why I was doing what I was doing. When she saw how the interest rate was much lower and that within two years, I would have it paid off, I knew she would be on board. Once I had paid off my credit card debt, I did the same for her credit card debt. Because I had explained the why to her, she was on board and knew the benefits of consolidating. Plus, it began to free our money up to be used for other areas, including savings. We had built up debt with our house working on various projects and realized we had had enough. We are currently working on paying off her debt, and any additional funds can be put towards paying it off early. Our situation may not be yours, but the point is to be honest, conversate, find the root of the problem, and work together to formulate a plan.

Once you commit to someone, you have invited them on your financial journey, and with any journey, you both need to be in sync with one another. Finances can rip apart even the strongest of relationships, and this was never going to be an option with us. We are a united front, and this would be no different. Communication was so important, and I could have easily done my own thing and told her this was what we needed to do. Even if it was 100% true, if I had not explained the why and showed her how this would benefit us, it may not have been as smooth a process. Not talking about your finances is not the way to go.

For the number of people who are too far apart on their financial beliefs, there are those that still find a way to work it out. Finances can end many relationships, whether it be couples, families, friends—you name it, it's happened. So how do people stay in a loving relationship and not let this destroy them? They make a plan and budget to ensure the bills that need to be paid are. After that, their money is their money.

One example I came across was a couple that had been married for a long time, had little debt, and yet their finances were separate. I asked how this worked as I was not sure the best way I would handle finances when I became married. The husband was a spender, and the wife was a saver. They were never going to change, but they decided this would not be what causes friction between them. They decided that the bills were to be paid each month, and the husband had to transfer half of the bills into their Bills Account, which the wife managed. Once he did so, he could do what he wanted with the remainder of his money. This worked for them because the bills were paid, she was able to save, and he could still spend—but there was some sort of budget placed on him, which at least reeled in some of his spending. Plus, he loved his wife and was willing to compromise. This was the key: He was willing to make changes for the marriage to work.

At the end of the day, it's up to you who you choose to share your life with, but you need to make sure to know the financial history of your partner because their debt can easily become your debt. And remember, sometimes a little change can go a long way!

Needs

This word is in direct crosshairs with another word we will speak about later: wants. These two words become interchangeable for many people and wreak havoc on your finances. My job is to explain the difference so you can distinguish between the two and not let your emotions make the decision for you.

My definition of **needs** is things you must have for quality of life, meaning without them, survival becomes difficult. When I say needs, I mean a roof over your head, food, water, electricity, clothing, and even transportation. Let's break a few of these down…

Stable Shelter. We all need a place to sleep where we feel secure and protected from the outside elements. It seems basic enough, right? Without a budget, this could turn into a major financial pitfall. It seems to be a consensus that 30% should be the most you pay for housing, but should you max it out? Do you need to live in the city where prices tend to be higher or move outside the city for something cheaper? Do you need to have roommates? Again, with a budget, you can see what you can afford so you can look at the right places. Just because your friends or colleagues live in a more expensive home does not mean you need to follow suit. You don't know their financial situation, and remember, your financial journey is not the same as theirs. Be smart and choose an area that fits your budget and allows you to continue to pay your other bills, debt, and, more importantly, your savings.

Vehicle. Depending on where you live, a car may be essential. If you live in a city with great public transportation, then having a car may not be a necessity, and those funds could be used elsewhere. But let's say a car is needed, and you need to buy one. What do you do? First, and you know what I'm about to say…review your budget! What car payment can you afford? Do you have money saved for a down payment? What does car insurance look like? How much is gas, and are there tolls? The car is just one piece of the financial puzzle.

There are many other considerations as described above. Just like we discussed previously, do your homework and research this before you shop for a car. If you don't, then the dealership will dictate your car, monthly payment, term, and other extras that could make the car far more expensive than it should be. Your first car most likely will not be your dream car, and if it is, you probably aren't reading this, so look for what will be reliable and suit your driving needs. Go in with the amount you want to spend (not the monthly payment, but the total amount), know what car you want to see, and if you need a loan, come in pre-approved if your financial institution has good car loan products. If you feel the dealership is pushing you past your financial comfort level, don't be afraid to walk away. You need to make sure that overall, the car, much like your home, will not be a debt that hurts your budget.

Food. There are two things to remember: groceries and going out to eat. Again, this should be a budget item, and this really needs to be prepared properly. If you are going to the store and buying food, that's great, and you are saving money rather than going out or ordering from home. But if you do not have a monetary plan and no list, you may be paying more than you thought and most likely throwing away your money. Budget, have a grocery list, and stick with it even if the store has everything buy-one-get-one-free. If it's not on the list or budget, then it stays out of the cart. This goes for online shopping as well, where clicking can be even easier, or you shop more often because it's convenient. Food is not getting cheaper and can cause a huge dent in your budget if you're not careful.

If you are going out, or ordering at home, you should have a budget for this as well. It's easy to go to the store, buy groceries, have the best of intentions, and then decide you don't want to cook. You're now spending money when you already have enough food at home, and there's a good chance you are ordering something you already have at home. Doesn't make sense. We try to pick certain nights where we eat out or order in and keep it as consistent as we can. It doesn't always work because life happens, but we have become much better than we were. It was easy to order or go out three or four times a week and even easier to convince ourselves that it made sense. It didn't help our budget, and it didn't help our waistline either (that's another topic altogether). But we had to make the changes together, and we did and have followed through, including me taking my lunch to work pretty much every day. Same as the housing and car—have a plan, stick with it, and it will help in so many ways.

I could continue on with clothing, furniture, cable, internet, anything that you would require to live or work. The issue is we want the best, and it's not that we don't deserve it, it's just what we are told we need isn't always true. Advertising alone can make the most trivial things seem mega important, and it's hard to separate what is a need and what is a want. In the end, it's going to be up to you as you know yourself better than anyone. As I have stated numerous times, I will not tell you what to do and will only give advice that I think will help. It's up to you to have the self-control to pull back on overspending on items you don't really need. Having a budget will help immensely, and if you stick with it, then you will have enough to get the things you need, save money, and be able to buy the things you want.

On-Time Payments

The plan is to make this a short chapter because this should be easy to explain. If you have any debt or money owed, such as phone, cable, utilities, etc., **make your payment on time, period.** I thought about ending the chapter and moving on but decided it would be best to go into it just a little bit more. There are two types of payments I want to discuss: loans and everyday bills.

Loans. You need a car and decide you want a loan because you reviewed your budget and found the right payment for you. You did the research, you stuck with your budget (maybe even went under the amount), and feel proud you did exactly what you should. Now you have an obligation to make your monthly (or bi-weekly) payments each month. This is part of the loan agreement you signed, and the due date should be consistent each month. It doesn't matter if you pay more; that monthly payment will be due each month. Pay it off faster if you can; just don't be late. And by late, I mean not paying for over thirty days. Your financial institution that holds the loan reports to the credit bureaus that you are making your payments on time, and when it's past thirty days, it hits your credit score hard. You are looking at an average of 50–70 points, which can be damaging.

If you do not have a system set up to make your payments (aka, a budget), then life can take over, and you could forget. It's not an excuse that will help you stop the damage to your credit from happening, but it's been a common theme. There are those who over-extended themselves and cannot afford the car, but we know there was no budget in place, and they were probably living a lifestyle they couldn't afford.

Let's say life happened, and you knew you would be a little late on your car payment. Now what? There should be a grace period that the lender has, meaning if you pay during this time span, you incur no penalties. But what if you may not be able to pay until after the grace period? The lender will have a late fee, which you could ask to have reversed, but this late fee is a much better option than incurring the hit on your credit. That 30 day late payment will be on your credit, and you will be answering why you were late for future lending needs. Remember to have a solid budget, put money aside for emergencies, buy a car you can afford, and this should help mitigate issues like this coming up.

Everyday Bills. These are not reported on your credit and are not considered debt, such as the above example. But you still need to make these payments on time as well to not incur late fees and hurt your credit. Yes, these do not show up on your credit report unless you owe them money and they report you.

Let's say you have your cell phone and decide you're done with your current company and go to cancel. You find out there's still a charge, but you refuse to pay it, thinking you're moving on and there's nothing they can do about it. This would be the wrong assumption because they still report to the credit bureaus if money is owed after thirty days, now affecting your credit like the previous example. And if you do not take care of this, it could go 60, 90, and even be sold to a collections agency, completely hurting your credit. Many times, someone does not know this has damaged their credit until they apply for another loan or even for utilities, insurance, or anything where a credit pull can occur. You now are deemed a risk, raising the down payment you have to put down or, even worse, not being approved.

This is your financial journey, and only you are responsible for it, so make sure you know what could happen based on your decisions. You are only hurting yourself.

Side note: If you feel you were charged in error, you can dispute with the company and see if they can correct it. If they can't, and they have reported it to the credit bureaus, you can dispute with them. Just make sure this does not occur when it is in collections status because now the debt has been sold, and you are dealing with another company. Pay your bills on time, and you can avoid that from happening.

Pay Yourself First (PYF)

This chapter will be a repeat, as **pay yourself first** has been mentioned numerous times. And yes, there may not be anything new you learn that hasn't already been read, but it shows how important this is to the success of your financial journey. To fully understand the PYF concept, we need to know the ramifications this had yesterday and will have today, tomorrow, and years from now.

Yesterday. What you haven't saved in the past means you will have more to make up for today to help fund tomorrow. Even if you have a budget, if this is not a category, then you're still putting yourself in the hole. If you get your first job at sixteen and you don't get serious about saving money until you're thirty, you have twelve years of missed opportunities. I'm not even talking about retirement plans, just budgeting some of your money into yourself. You've put yourself behind in case of emergencies, saving for a car, vacations, even potentially losing your job. And what happens when you do not have any savings and need financial help? You tend to use credit and over-extend yourself, making it even harder to save. Start as soon as you can, even before a job, with money earned from holidays, birthdays, chores—whatever you can do to make sure yesterday doesn't impede today and tomorrow.

Today. You have the choice to stop the cycle of never having money when financial situations arise or being able to do the things you enjoy. If you have not been saving, then today is the day to start. Get that budget out, review your money coming in, put in your monthly expenses (review and have a plan if it's more than what you take in), and find the room to PYF. I've said this previously: it's about building the habit, not the amount to start. So if you can only put away a small amount, then do it. Find out what your floor is and make sure you never save less than that each month. Be aggressive if you can but do not put money aside that you know you will need to cover your monthly bills. It will defeat the purpose and make you doubt you can accomplish this. If it seems too much, go online to read what financial experts think (make sure it fits what is best for your financial plan), or see your financial institution and sit down with them. The resources are there, and this is not the time to feel embarrassed. Instead, think of it as the first step to make your tomorrow that much brighter.

Tomorrow. You realize the years you were not saving and see what you have lost. But instead of feeling down, you followed the steps of today, and now here we are in tomorrow. You feel confident, you have a plan, and you can see the positive impact this has on your financial journey. You haven't put together an unrealistic plan and have made the changes in your budget to start your savings with an amount that will not impact your other financial obligations. These are the days where you start seeing the money grow, you rely on less debt, being able to use cash instead of credit for emergencies, and overall building your financial future. You have made a positive change that will continue to fuel your tomorrows each day.

Years from Now. You did it—you maintained your dedication to savings, you've been able to increase your amount as you have paid down debt, gotten those raises, and kept the Pay Yourself First mentality a top priority in your financial journey! Between your retirement (401k, IRAs, etc.), you can enter the world of retirement and enjoy all the hard work that got you there. Now don't be mistaken; you were able to have fun during the past years as you have saved for your vacations, house, marriage, kids, etc., so you stayed the course, and you enjoyed every step along your financial journey as you got closer to retirement. You've earned it, and that day where you decided enough was enough will forever be the day you took control of your finances and made sure you could live the life you wanted moving forward. It wasn't easy, but you were focused, and now you can really savor this moment. Your financial journey never really ends, but you have made every provision to make it as easy as possible right now.

Questions (Ask Them!)

By now, the idea that this is your financial journey should be second nature. What works best for you and your financial plan needs to be your focus. You have your budget ready to go, including paying yourself, and now you're ready for whatever the next step might be. Now it's time to decide what financial solutions work best for your financial plan. The research is at the tip of your fingers, and you can search the endless information from local accounts to online accounts on where you want to put your money or look for a lender. This is great and will narrow down who you want to be your banking partner. But, before you dive headfirst, it's good to ask any **questions** you may have, even if you think they may sound silly. The reason is you need to understand all there is with that financial institution, the accounts, and the expectations you have as a client. I break this down into two sections: checking/savings accounts and loans.

Checking and Savings Accounts. You need to know what fees there may be, what interest rates are, if they will make changes based on balances, how often you can use the accounts, if the financial institution is rated highly, and more importantly, are they there to be a resource for your financial journey? As we discussed in Chapter F, all financial institutions pretty much offer similar products, and the regulations are the same. What you want to know is how fee-driven they are and what they offer outside of their accounts. Do they have financial literacy courses in person or online, and will they want to take the time to help you with your next step? Financial institutions are great to offer short-term bonus rates or give you money to open an account with them, and in the beginning, it'll be a great partnership. What happens once the honeymoon period is over? Are you still an individual they want to help even when you may not be someone that can do more than just open a checking and savings account? Or will you just feel like you are bothering them when you need answers to help you maintain your financial plan? Ask and find out because you need to know, and if it starts out great but quickly goes downhill, you need to find another place that wants to be your long-term financial partner, not just make their numbers look good.

Loans. This is even more important to ask questions. There are lenders who will put you into a loan that is not right for you, but it's right for them. An example is a car dealership where you go in, and they look for financing. They may not always go to the financial institution that is offering the best rate, but the one that gives them the higher fee back. It's unfortunate, but you need to go into this understanding that the only one looking out for you is you. Now there are many lenders, and I have worked at some, that truly want to ensure you are in the best loan that will not cause you financial hardship. In the end, you are still signing a document that states you are being lent X amount of money and you agree to pay back by a certain date. My best advice is to ask questions and ask more questions and if it does not make sense, ask more questions. People who want to help you be in the best possible financial situation will take the time to help you understand. Those that don't will rush you, make you feel stupid, and force you into their best deal. Don't allow them to do this, no matter how much you may need or want the funds for. Be prepared to walk away and shop around; it's your right as the consumer. Once you know you will be taking on this financial obligation, after making sure it fits your budget, then you need to make sure you are in the right loan that makes this a reality.

In the end, this is your financial journey and yours alone, so you are in control and no one else. When decisions that involve your money are in front of you, understand the account/loan so when you sign any documents, you know this fits exactly what you want. Never be afraid to ask questions to understand fully what is being offered to you—never! You are in control, and you've gotten this far. You don't need someone trying to force you into something that will impede all the progress you have made on your financial journey.

Retirement

I do not have many regrets, as I feel each negative experience helped mold me into the person I am today, and I hope it's been for the better. Although, there is one moment I continue to kick myself for being so naïve and thinking I knew better than I did.

When I was in my early twenties, I had my first job that offered a 401k plan, and I decided that I could not afford to contribute any of my hard-earned money toward it. Even though my company matched up to 4%, and it would be pre-tax when the money came out of my paycheck, I said no. Basically, I could have chosen to receive free money from my company and start my road to early **retirement** (I told myself I would retire early but chose not to do one of the most basic steps to start this). Yep, I was the person I gave as an example, and when I think of the six years I contributed nothing, and what I would have had now, it literally makes me want to cry in frustration. Yes, I did not have a budget set up, and so, of course, I couldn't see where this would make sense. Four percent of my salary would be nothing when I really look at it, and I wish I could go back and get my younger self to listen. But as we have spoken about throughout this journey, we all make financial mistakes, and the important thing is we recognize them, we learn, and we make sure we don't make those same mistakes. We especially want to help others, which is why I always tell students to start contributing as soon as they work for a company that has a 401k, especially if they have matching funds.

Before I continue with this chapter, I will not be giving any advice on investments. Any questions need to be with a licensed financial advisor who has the expertise to discuss these products. Your financial institution should have financial advisors, and more importantly, the brokerage firm your company uses for their 401k will have financial advisors for you to speak to. This is an area you really need to speak with the right person who is licensed with the state and can hold these conversations. There are too many issues if you receive the wrong advice from someone who is not licensed and you are not protected through the state they work in. Just like anything else, interview two or three advisors and see who is best for your financial journey, and don't be afraid to see if they have had any issues reported to the state from other clients.

What if you work with a company that does not have a 401k, and you want to start preparing for retirement? Individual Retirement Accounts (IRAs) would be a great option to contribute to each paycheck. These are designed as long-term financial strategies and would also be a great compliment for any retirement plan. Now, when it comes to where to put the funds, you need to speak with a financial advisor that can put together a plan that fits your current goals, budget, and risk. You need to know what is out there, and with an ever-changing financial environment, you need to have an expert at your side. This may seem very straightforward, and it's meant to be.

The sooner you start putting in money for your retirement, the more you will accumulate if you have the right plan. It's your financial journey; however, it's good to have the right resources with you to help guide you where you need to be. I would advise speaking with an advisor through your financial institution, employer, or someone in your circle you trust (make sure you listen to someone you believe has their own finances in order). I don't want to get too involved as there are so many paths investing can lead, and I do not want to lead you into any potential advice I am not licensed for. I feel this is where many get in trouble. Besides, what may be the right investment for me, may not be for you.

Surround Yourself with the Right People

This chapter is not stating you need to surround yourself with all like-minded people because I do not agree with this. It's good to have a variety of different thoughts, backgrounds, anything that can help you grow. It's the old saying of if you are the smartest person within your group, it's time for a new group. I think this is an extreme, but there are some points we can take from this saying, the most important being: **surround yourself with the right people!**

If your group of friends spend whenever they want, do not have a budget, and put most of their purchases on credit cards with no plan to pay them off, it's going to be difficult. You may be the one they call cheap, or you never want to have fun, or that you don't live in the moment. All solid reasons to spend, spend, spend—except for one detail. Eventually, you hit the wall of debt and cannot do anything else. Not having a financial plan will catch up with you, and you need to remain focused. It doesn't mean you cannot have fun. It just means you need to ensure this purchase today will not be a financial burden tomorrow. Unless your friends have unlimited resources at their disposal, then the wall is just around the corner. And if you have friends that do have unlimited resources, you will just be trying to keep up with them and will end up hitting that wall.

Does this mean you need to make all new friends? Of course not. It just means you need to have a balance. Make sure you also have people who share in wanting to better their financial future and who want to make sacrifices today that will allow them financial freedom down the road. When your friends are making that last-second trip out of town, having support will make it easier to say no and not feel like you're being left out. Having a network of support is helpful and can make your financial journey smoother and easier to stay on track. They want to have fun, too, just not at the expense of their financial plan. Plus, it's a great way to share tips on what has worked for them and ways you could continue to improve your financial journey. Remember, it's a fluid journey with many changes, so make sure you can adapt when needed.

Now, I don't want you to be that friend that preaches to their friends who spends as soon as they can. No one wants that person constantly telling them how much smarter they are when it comes to finances. You hear this a lot, and from the beginning, I am not the all knowing financial guru or someone that has all of the answers. I have made mistakes and continue to grow and learn. I want to be someone that you can speak to and someone who listens. Advice isn't always needed and many times is not what people want. If I speak with someone and feel they are judging me and before I am finished, they cannot wait to tell me what they would do, I tend to shut down, and I feel many are the same way.

Be there for your friends if they need you and if the time comes when they are ready to start their financial journey. You can be a resource for them to help them build what will work for their financial situation. Do not force them and judge their decisions. After all, it's their life and their journey. You know how difficult it is when you realize what you have been doing is affecting your financial future. Think of the people who helped you and be that person; it will be a breath of fresh air from a judgmental environment.

I will also warn you that there could be a situation where someone you are close to hits that wall of debt and comes to you not for advice, but for money. You are the only one who can decide what to do, and I couldn't possibly begin to put myself in your shoes. I will just leave a couple of thoughts to mull over: Will this affect your financial plan to the point it could cause hardship in the future? Do you trust this person would pay you back if that's the decision you make? It's a tough call, but you always need to make sure you are looking out for yourself and not causing any financial consequences. It may sound harsh, but the reality is what it is. I would rather deal with the worst-case scenarios so you are prepared. I have seen friendships end because of money, and I can bet many relationships as well when money is borrowed.

In the end, it's your decision, and whatever you decide is what you decide. Just make sure, like everything else we have spoken about, that you have all the facts to make the best-informed decision for you.

Taxes

This will be the shortest chapter in the book. I have one piece of advice: Speak to an expert on **taxes**. When you are first starting out in your career, you may not need a tax professional and can do the online tax filing. I did for many years. However, you will most likely start to accumulate assets such as a home, vehicles, retirement accounts, and many others where having a tax professional will be invaluable. Information on taxes can change quickly, and you may not even know if it will or has affected you unless you are part of the industry. Make sure you have an expert on your side to file your taxes correctly so you avoid any possible issues with the IRS. And if you do, have someone who can go to bat for you. Interview two or three tax professionals and see who fits you the best and find out all you can. This is someone you may be working with for many years, and having a trusted tax professional is invaluable.

See, I told you this would be quick!

Utilize Online Tools

We discussed some of these previously when speaking about financial institutions. There are numerous ways you can keep yourself on track in almost every aspect of your financial journey. The tools available are at your fingertips and can help you track your daily and monthly progress. Here are a few areas where **online tools can be helpful.**

Budgets. Excel is a great place to start your budget and allows various options based on where you are in your current financial journey. This needs to be the first online tool to get sorted, and if you do not see what you want, Google budget templates and see what you find.

Tracking Spending. You want to get a bit more complex with this one, and your financial institution is a perfect place to start. Ask about their money management programs through their online banking to get started. You can have various options outside of your financial institution, but the point is to know where your money is going in real time.

Paying Debt. Your budget will get your plan started, but you need to know where you are at. The above programs will help but have the companies you have your debt with on your phone. Download the apps and monitor these so you can see the debt coming down. It's a motivational tool along with a convenient way to make your payment.

Credit Report. Your financial institution and/or credit card companies may already have an online tool they use or partner with. Try these first, but you can always use other tools such as Credit Karma or other associated platforms. You can always pull your credit report each year with the three major bureaus, and they have many tools to track your credit as well. Remember, if you want your true credit score, there usually is a cost.

E-Alerts. Use your online banking platforms for any financial institution you have accounts in. These are part of your account and will allow you to monitor your money and catch potential fraud. Set up e-alerts to help you stay current on any activity you want to know about. Want to keep a certain balance in your checking? Set up an e-alert to notify you if your balance goes under a certain amount. There are many options, so choose what's important to you.

If you can think of it, there is most likely an online function that corresponds to it. It's a great time to be able to check your financial journey whenever you want it, right on your phone. If you want to be more old school, you can always write down what you spend to keep track along with your budget. There is no wrong way. Just make sure it allows you to stay focused!

Vacations

I tend to speak more on subjects I have had personal issues with, and **vacations** are no exception. I was the example of putting the trip on my credit card and taking a long time to pay it off, usually incurring additional expenses while paying the card off.

My low point came when I had taken a trip and put about $600 on my credit card, and it took over two years to pay it off! I was making a decent salary, but I had no budget to speak of, and the money went out just as fast as it came in. I didn't have people around me to show me another way, or I was too stubborn to listen (my parents would have made sure to let me know what I was doing made no sense). So a weekend trip cost me much more than originally thought when you add interest, and of course, I am positive there were some late payments there. At one point, I owed more than the limit on the card. I don't look back as if the trip wasn't fun, because it was, but I ended up paying for the fun for more than two years and dug myself into a hole that took a while to get out of. Plus, this was the time I was not contributing to my 401k, so I had no financial plan at all. When I look back, I realize that with just some simple budgeting, I could have made much better decisions and not put myself into debt for one weekend trip. I was fortunate enough to learn and realize where my financial hiccups occurred, and they all start with a basic budget.

I love to travel, and so does my wife, and we make sure when we do that, we have the money to pay for it. I do use my credit card to pay for hotels and flights, partially for the rewards but also for security. If there were any issues, I prefer not to have the card linked to my bank accounts. Before, I used the card just so I could afford the trip, not for security and definitely not because I had the money (plus, points don't really help when you are in a financial hole). We now budget the money and pay the card back either immediately or when we are back home, depending on the length of time between purchase and taking the trip. I took my wife to New York for our wedding anniversary and paid for it in October, and we went at the end of the year. I had the trip paid off before the plane took off, leaving me feeling good about not worrying about debt and being able to truly enjoy myself. The sense of relief knowing you won't come home to massive debt makes each vacation even better, and I am happy I finally learned my lesson. And as I said earlier, I had to make this revelation and no one else. Once I did, got a plan, and really took my financial journey seriously, every trip has been an excellent retreat!

Wants

We discussed **wants** in the Needs chapter, so I do not want to repeat too much of what has already been said. I do want to emphasize the importance that if you want to purchase something that is not part of your day-to-day living needs, there is nothing wrong with this. Just make sure you follow your budget or have set aside funds for this purchase.

Everyone I know has things they like to treat themselves to that could include shoes, food, trips, concerts, sporting events—anything that you enjoy having or doing. And that's great! You should look to put money aside for the things you enjoy so you can enjoy your life. In the beginning, this may not be an option as you learn to navigate your financial journey, but in time, you will be able to reap the benefits of your tireless focus. We have one life (as far as we know), and we should enjoy it to the fullest without affecting our future.

You can definitely be financially responsible and still have fun; you don't have to deal with absolutes.

The person telling you that your money doesn't go with you when you die is correct, but I would rather live my life being financially comfortable than stressing about the mounting debt being accumulated. The same goes for anyone who makes you feel guilty for enjoying yourself based on how you purchase items or if you do not use their advice.

In the end, you know yourself best, and your financial journey is yours and yours alone, so create it just for you. Be smart, stick with your financial plan, and you will see positive results before you know it. And if you stumble, then go back, review your financial plan, and move forward. As long as you do not get yourself into a situation that creates an immediate negative impact on your finances—and your life—then you will be able to move forward and learn from this.

My wife and I had a hiccup with a sporting event we wanted to see, and we paid a decent amount for two tickets. The seats were okay, and the day before, one of our friends had even better seats available if we wanted them. We decided to buy them and look to sell the other tickets, banking on the fact we would be able to. On the day of the game, we got to the stadium to meet our friends, as we had a few hours before the game. Okay, fine, we were tailgating. I went online to sell them, and first, the internet connection was horrible, which made sense since there were over 60,000 people around the stadium. Then, and we still do not know how we accomplished this, we somehow lost our virtual tickets. We still had the upgraded tickets, which meant we didn't miss the game, but we now had tickets we could not sell, so that was a loss. When we went inside the stadium and sat down, we were happy where we were and enjoyed the game, but the total experience cost us double what we had originally paid. This was a classic case of wanting to sit in better seats and it not being a necessity but a very costly want.

The point I am trying to make is that no one is perfect. We hear from people that they never have any issues and they make no money mistakes, and maybe that is true for some, as I do not know their circumstances. But for most of us, we will have these from time to time, but based on our financial plan, we are able to move on, learning not to be greedy just because an opportunity presents itself. The same goes for you. Have your plan and keep at it, even when you have a hiccup moment. Learn from it and move forward, and do not let anyone make you feel like less of a person.

X Marks the Spot

'm not going to lie; these last few letters were not easy to think of topics for, and when I set out to write this book, I really didn't know what X, Y, and Z would be called. But as I was writing, it started to become clear what this chapter would be and how the book would end. From here on out, it's more of helping you realize what you are capable of and that you can control and find success in your financial future. So let's start the last three chapters with a bang!

We have all read about pirate maps where the treasure is buried where X is marked. **X marks the spot** is basically the way to get from point A to point B, with B being a lot of money, gold, valuable art, anything that was worth burying, and making sure only yourself, or very few people, knew about it.

Think about your financial journey as your own treasure map in the making. When you make the commitment to start this financial journey, this becomes your Point A, and your financial journey becomes your treasure map. Since we are all different in where we see ourselves, Point B is whatever goals you have set for yourself. It could be any financial goal such as being debt-free, having six months saved, being ready for retirement, etc. Whatever goal you have for your financial journey has become your own personal treasure map. You could even have several treasure maps, and once you complete your financial goal, maybe you're ready for the next one.

The best part? It's yours and yours alone (unless you and your partner create one, and then it's a shared win)! So start today, get your budget together, and find out where you want to be financially, and start your treasure map. This will be one of the most rewarding journeys in your life, and the treasure at the end will be well worth the journey!

Yes, You Can!

Yes, you can! When we embark on any journey, there will be doubts. There will be people who say you're doing it wrong, or what's the point in the end. Do not listen to them. Use their words as fuel to continue your financial journey.

Everything we do that has the potential to change our lives for the positive will always be tough. Life itself will come up and potentially knock you down and even pause your journey, but do not let up. The plan you created was built to be able to adapt and change where needed, as long as you continue to move forward. If this was easy, then we would all be financially comfortable, and you would have no need for this book or any of the gurus out there. Find what works best for you and incorporate this into your financial plan. It needs to be something that is for you because you know yourself better than anyone else does.

I said at the beginning of this book that you may not find each chapter relevant, and that's alright. Take what you need and use it if it helps, and if you find one of the chapters seems to be relevant later on, then use what you need. I've found that people want you to follow their advice even if it doesn't seem to work for you, and that can lead to frustration, and that is not what this is about. The truth is you are here and ready to really start your financial plan. Heck, you even made it to the end of the book! This critical first step should make you feel confident and secure that you are doing the right thing for yourself. You know it won't be easy because life isn't easy, but you know in the end you will be setting up yourself, your partner, and your family for a very bright and successful future. So the question you need to ask yourself is, can you do it?

Yes, you can!

Zenith

I Googled the word zenith, and it came up as "the time at which something is most powerful and successful." I thought this was the only way to end this book with this word, which also completes the alphabet.

You may have decided to take this book and start your financial journey. You may already be in the middle of it and are always looking for ways to continue your success. Or maybe a life event has happened where you need to adjust. It does not matter. You are doing something powerful to make your financial future successful. Keep this in mind when the journey becomes difficult, and remember why you are doing this in the first place.

We all want to have the best life we can, and being financially comfortable should be a goal for all of us. What that actually means will differ from one person to the next, as it should be. We each have our reasons for starting and what we see at the end. The one common theme is we each see a better financial future by doing this.

I appreciate you taking the time to read this book, as it was one of the greatest joys I have found in writing this. I truly believe everyone should continue to learn no matter what stage they are in. Once we think we know everything on a subject, we become complacent, and this is when we get in trouble, even when giving others advice. The financial world is constantly evolving, and I ask you to always be open to new ideas that can benefit your financial journey. I continue to do the same, and as I said in the very beginning, I am by no means the end-all-be-all for financial literacy, just someone who sees the importance of financial literacy and the impact this can have on so many people.

Thank you again, and I hope you found the information helpful as you continue your own personal financial journey. Good luck and stay the course!